Wood Appliqué

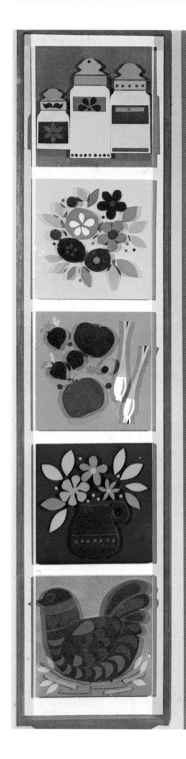
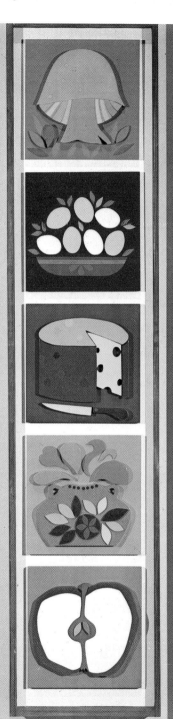

C-1

Wood Appliqué

Jean Ray Laury

VAN NOSTRAND REINHOLD COMPANY
New York Cincinnati Toronto London Melbourne

To my Mother

Acknowledgments

I am grateful to architect Alexander Girard for his cut wood designs, and to designer Norman Laliberté for his painted wooden images. Each has been a great inspiration to me.

I am also grateful to my mother, Mrs. Alice Ray, who always let me (as a child) use whatever saws, paints, and scrap wood could be found in the basement or garage. She always admired the results of my efforts without making an issue of any mess.

I thank Gayle Smalley for the many times she packed lights, camera gear, and dog into her car to do the patient and meticulous photographic work, as well as Stan Bitters and Tom Hurley for their willingness to photograph anywhere at any hour. I particularly thank Frank B. Laury who carefully read and advised me with the manuscript.

Ruth Law, Patricia Hopper, Joyce Aiken, and Marlo Johansen have generously loaned numerous pieces of work. Their talents and humor enirch the pages of this book. Last, I thank my daughter Lizabeth Laury for loaning her first work in wood.

Van Nostrand Reinhold Company Regional Offices:
New York Cincinnati Chicago Millbrae Dallas
Van Nostrand Reinhold Company International Offices:
London Toronto Melbourne

Copyright © 1973 by Litton Educational Publishing, Inc.
Library of Congress Catalog Card Number 72-9707
ISBN 0-442-24695-1

Photographs by Gayle Smalley
and Stan Bennett, Stan Bitters, Tom Hurley,
Frank B. Laury

Designed by Rosa Delia Vasquez

Published by Van Nostrand Reinhold Company
450 West 33rd Street, New York, N.Y. 10001
Published simultaneously in Canada by
Van Nostrand Reinhold Limited

16 15 14 13 12 11 10 9 8 7 6 5 4 3 2 1

Figure I-1. "Moon."

Figure I-2. "Hand."

Figure C-1. "Foods." Each panel is 12 inches wide by 56 inches high. Designs are cut from white pine and then enameled and decorated. Individual squares are appliquéd to vertical plywood panels. By Joyce Aiken and Jean Ray Laury.

Figure I-3. "Ummm," 10 inches by 12 inches. An old board, with weathered nail holes showing at the end, was cut and glued to a felt background.

Figure I-4. "Pear," 7½ inches by 9½ inches. Cut and painted wood is applied to a stained mahogany panel.

Contents

Figure I-5. "Help," 8 inches by 10 inches. Thin weathered wood was cut and reassembled with colored felt.

Introduction

Almost any family garage, toolroom, or workshop will have everything you need to complete many of the projects shown in this book. All are made from wood, most in the form of boards. A small saw is needed, as well as a variety of paints and stains for color. A simple line drawing, transferred to wood, emerges as a three-dimensional form. It is exciting for children (and no less exciting for adults) to see their sketches turn into animals, or creatures, or other objects which have form and weight, and which can be moved about or played with. You'll find your children (as well as your friends) fascinated by the activity and the results of your work.

It is not necessary to have a garage or a toolshop to devote to your woodwork. If the kitchen is available, use it. If there's more space in the dining-room, cover the table and work there. A sheet of plywood placed over a table not only protects the table surface, but gives you a larger working area. Nobody notices the little collections of sawdust on the floor if there is something colorful and creative on the table. You need only decide if the house is for you to *use*, or if it must be reserved only for viewing. Let your home adjust to your activities rather than adjust your activities to your home. Decide what you want to do, and your home will offer the means. Of course, you don't have to use the dining-room. A porch or a laundry room will do as well.

Your one basic and essential tool is a saw. The simplest of these is a coping saw, Figure I-7. It is easy to use, safe, and inexpensive. 'Since its blade is very narrow, it allows you to cut curves and corners easily.

The most valuable piece of equipment to own for cutting decorative wood pieces is a small electric jigsaw (such as a Dremel Moto-shop saw). The jigsaw is sometimes referred to as a scroll saw. The Dremel saw is lighter in weight and less expensive that a standard jigsaw, although it costs more than a coping saw (Figure I-8). If you become engrossed in this work, you will need it. Since it is lightweight, it can easily be carried in one hand to the kitchen counter, where you can plug it in for use. The counter makes a good working surface at a comfortable height. I find this saw as essential as a food mixer to homemaking. Anyone who can handle an electric can opener or an electric knife can handle this saw.

Figure I-6. ''Nostalgia Box,'' 11 inches by 21 inches. Both natural forms and painted objects are displayed in this collection of ready-made boxes.

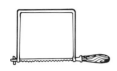

Figure 1-7. The coping saw is safe, easy to use, and costs little. Many of the projects shown in this book can be made with just this one saw.

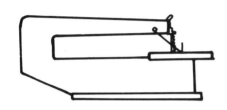

Figure I-8. The electric jigsaw will greatly speed up the wood cutting. It is simple to operate, and can be moved with ease.

While there is an excellent finger guard on most jigsaws, the tool is not a dangerous one. My daughter started sawing out her own toys and horses with this saw when she was four years old. As a designer, I have found the saw to be an indispensable shop tool in producing large-scale work. As a homemaker, I have found it a joy to use in making cutouts for the kitchen, or puzzles out of children's drawings.

For large-scale work, a band saw is helpful but not essential. Its primary advantage is its speed and its ability to cut thicker pieces of wood. If it is necessary to select one tool above all the others, certainly the small electric jigsaw is the most versatile for home use. Its base tilts so that angles can be cut. The very narrow blade allows for the cutting of intricate and tiny shapes.

Wood has had an irresistible appeal throughout the world. It has been used by almost every culture to produce tools and articles of beauty and utility. Because it is a natural material — a living one — it has both strength and character and yet remains yielding. The colors and textures are varied, and it comes in many different forms. But even in the form of boards, we have an incredible variety from which to choose.

Glass, steel, stucco, and synthetics have become more and more common in our homes, and as they replace wood, they increase our need to feel the warmth of wood in our everyday environment. With great pleasure and pride, wooden spoons and tools are hung on the wall or displayed bouquet-like in bowls while we put the stainless steel mixing spoons into a drawer. So appealing is the surface of wood that it has many imitators. Steel and plastic are often given a surface coat of paint that imitates wood. Vinyls and contact papers are made to look like wood. They lack the smell and texture and softness of wood, but they are an attempt to recapture something we miss. We feel cheated when we touch what appears to be wood, only to have our fingers encounter glassy smooth resin or vinyl-covered steel.

Wood need not be new to be usable or beautiful. Some of the very best woods are those which have been aged through use and weathering. As you walk or ride your bike or the bus, watch for fences being torn down, or stacked wood boxes, or a friendly farmer with a scrap pile of wood. These scrap woods will be one of your best sources.

All the projects shown here use wood in the form of boards, since boards are easy to obtain, ready to use, and can be cut and painted with a minimum of tools or difficulty. Simple tools and scrap woods make possible a tremendous range of projects. The ones shown here offer a beginning, suggesting some of the various directions your work might take. Your imagination, need, invention, and humor will lead you from here into your own style and methods.

Stains and Paints

There are just two basic ways of adding color to wood. The first — a stain — takes advantage of the wood as a base color and adds to it, changes it, or intensifies it. The second — paint — covers the wood with an opaque surface, adding a layer of color.

Before the addition of any color there is a tremendous variation in the natural hues of woods. Redwood, when aged, turns a silver gray or deep umber. New, it is a deep reddish brown. Pine, which is an almost white wood, yellows and darkens gradually with age. Untreated woods change, and the original color of the wood will affect stains or thinned paints. Wood color does not affect the color of opaque paints. In using any of the stains or paints, *always* read the labels on the containers. Read the labels before purchasing, and then read the directions on the spray or paint cans before using them. Most labels will specify the correct solvent or thinner to be used.

Water-Base Paint

Paints and stains may be water base, and these include latex, tempera, acrylic, watercolor, some dyes, and marking pens. One of the primary advantages of their use is that brushes, hands, and spilled paints may be cleaned with water. This makes them practical for children (or inexperienced adults). Latex and acrylic will dry to a permanent finish, but others (such as tempera) will not. Those which are not permanent can be covered with a protective spray — shellac, a plastic spray, or clear varnish — to keep colors from rubbing off with handling or use.

Oil-Base Paint

Enamels, artist's oil colors, oil stains, and many household paints have an oil base. These may be thinned with turpentine or paint thinner to make stains that can be wiped directly onto the wood. It is best to start with a light stain, adding more color or more layers as needed. Paint thinner or turpentine should be put into a container (a tuna-fish can works well). Add some paint or color to the thinner and stir. Then dip a folded cloth, or a brush, into the mixture and wipe, or brush, it onto a piece of the scrap wood to determine if the color is right. Remember that when the stain dries, the color may change slightly. When your color sample satisfies you, wipe the moistened cloth or brush over the entire surface of your wood to remove any excess.

If colors are to be opaque, with a bright smooth finish, the wood must first be given some attention. Sanding is the first step in order to remove any burrs and rough areas from the wood. Then a layer of undercoat is painted onto the wood to seal and further smooth it. When dry (check the directions on the can for proper drying time), use a fine sandpaper over the undercoat. If the wood appears to be perfectly smooth, wipe the surface with a dampened cloth to remove all dust particles. It is now ready for enameling. If the wood was very open-grained, or if you were too enthusiastic in your sanding and removed the undercoat, you may have to add another layer. Repeat the sanding. Wood may also be sealed with shellac or wood sealer. The sealer (whether you use undercoat or shellac) must be sanded to a smooth finish.

Finally, when sanding is completed and the surface feels smooth, wipe again with a dampened cloth. All dust and lint particles must be removed, or they will mar the surface of the enamel.

Figure I-9. "Bird," 8 inches by 9 inches. Detail of cut weathered board. Wood is left un-painted and unstained.

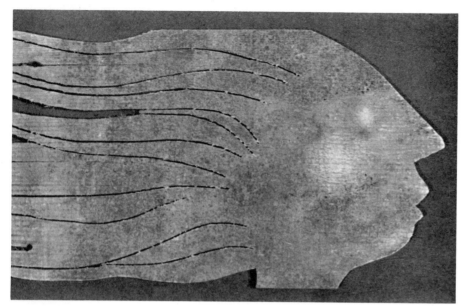

Figure I-10. "Girl in the Wind," 8 inches by 11½ inches. The girl's face emerges from the board with a minimum of cutting. Rubbed chalk suggests the eye and cheek.

Spray Paints

Spray cans offer a tremendous advantage in painting wood. They come in a beautiful range of colors, and they are available as enamels, lacquers, opaque paints, transparent colors, and candy-apple lacquers. To use spray paints, you must treat the wood as described above — by undercoating and sanding.

Although paints in spray cans are more expensive than paints bought in regular cans, they are also easier to use. They eliminate the need for brushes and paint thinner, and they don't dry out as a can of paint sometimes does if the lid is not on tight.

Spray nozzles sometimes cause problems. After spraying, turn the can upside down, pressing the nozzle until the spray comes out clear (as directed on the can). This should clear the nozzle. Or remove the nozzle after spraying and drop it into a small container (a baby-food jar works well) of paint or lacquer thinner. This will keep the nozzle clear and ready for use next time. Keep one or two of the nozzles from empty spray cans so that you have a replacement for an occasional defective nozzle.

Use spray paint in a large, well-ventilated area. Out-of-doors works well unless it's windy. Then dust may become a problem. Place your cut wood pieces on an overturned cardboard box to spray paint them. Be sure you do not inadvertently spray your picnic table, patio, or fence. Spray paints need space!

No Paint?

If you have no paints available (and the stores have closed for the night or weekend, and you are suddenly inspired and *must* work), look around the house. Food coloring, while not permanent, will add a good color stain, especially to untreated light woods. A finish spray coat of lacquer or plastic varnish will help retain the color. Shoe polish makes a great stain, especially the dye and shine variety. Any shoe dye or leather stain will do. Household liquids, such as grape juice, wine, or bleach, will lighten or darken woods. Chalks, showcard paint, and children's tempera offer brilliant colors, although again a sealer will be needed over the paint.

The coloring agent helps to determine the finished surface of the wood. The method you use depends upon the result you wish to achieve. There is no way to get an opaque, smooth, shiny colored surface without sanding, undercoating, and enameling. However, if you prefer to retain the grain and pattern of the wood, then there is no better way than to use a stain. Either is an appropriate way to work with wood.

The following chapters suggest various projects that are possible with cutting and painting wood. Sometimes the cut and painted pieces are appliquéd to another piece of wood, and this process may be referred to as wood appliqué.

For those readers who may have reservations about woodwork, I assure you that the procedures are simple, requiring no formal training in shop or woodworking. It is actually very similar to fabric collage — if you just substitute a saw for a scissors. Most of the work in this book was produced by women with no background in shop or in industrial arts. Patricia Hopper, whose hardwood doors are shown in Figure 4-20, was a political science major, and she is now a full-time designer. Ruth Law, a toy maker whose painted wood objects appear in Chapter 3, was graduated in biology. Joyce Aiken, who collaborated with me on many of the works shown in this book, received her graduate degree in education. We still claim ten fingers. Apiece!

Few activities will bring you more pleasure than woodwork. Whether you wood-appliqué your front door, or decorate the mixing spoons in your kitchen, the results are shared by all those who are around you. The work becomes a part of your personal environment. This book will introduce you to the fun, and challenge, and satisfaction of working with wood.

Figure 1-1. "Hawk," 8 inches by 9½ inches.
Simple cutout of untreated weathered wood.
By Jean Ray Laury.

1. Small Projects

A good first project is one which lets you finish a panel without too great an investment in energy, time, or money. It should take you through the processes without obligating you to six weeks of work. A one-day, or one-evening, project seems a more exciting beginning.

Any wood which requires no finish will, of course, simplify everything. Just cut and use natural wood, letting color then be added to the background. "Dove" in Figure C-5 (page 19) is a good example of minimum wood finish. Color is added through the felts used as backing, and the wood itself is left unfinished except for staining. A panel of this size and complexity can easily be finished between lunch and the 5 o'clock news.

A lumberyard (especially the do-it-yourself kind) is your best initial source of wood. Clear pine, ½-inch thick, is available almost anywhere, and it is one of the easiest woods to cut and paint. These boards come in various widths. Wood just ¼-inch thick is even easier to saw, but it is sometimes hard to find, even in lumberyards. It is, however, commonly used in boxes, and it is sometimes sold as "boxwood." If you have access to old apple boxes, orange crates, fruit-drying trays, or sometimes old outbuildings and fences, this wood is excellent for small panels. It is thin and soft, and very detailed shapes are easily cut. Another panel cut from weathered wood, in this case ¼-inch thick, is shown in Figure 1-1.

A grocery store or a liquor store will occasionally let you have wood boxes. Cleaning out a basement or an attic may yield a surprising supply of this thin wood. Discarded small structures may provide good supplies, as such thin wood is often used to make them lightweight. Rabbit hutches, chicken sheds, and similar buildings yield surprisingly beautiful weathered wood. Shingles, especially old ones, may be used, although they vary in thickness from one end to the other. Houses or buildings in the path of reconstruction developments yield tremendous quantities, but you should always seek permission *before* taking any of this wood. Buildings under construction often have around them great quantities of wood in small pieces. Salvage companies have such materials sorted and stacked. But finding the wood may, in itself, be an adventure.

You can, of course, order any wood you choose. It can be milled to whatever thickness you specify. This adds to the cost, although it assures you of having precisely the wood you want or need. It becomes a matter of which you run short of first — time or money. For most beginning cut-wood projects, the standard clear white pine available from a lumberyard is your best buy. If you are not familiar with what most lumberyards have to offer, browse through the supplies so that you will know what is available. Be careful not to substitute fir for pine, since it is usually full of resin and is exceptionally hard. Plywood is not very satisfactory for the cut woodwork. The surface is difficult to smooth with sanding, and the cut edges often have small openings that require filling.

A felt-covered panel makes an excellent background for the cut wood. It adds color and eliminates painting. First determine the size of your panel. This may be decided by the size of your cut wood design — if you have already cut it. Or it may be determined by the area in which you are going to hang, or use, the finished piece. Whichever it is, you need to cut the background wood to the finished size. Plywood makes an excellent material for this since it is readily available, comes in any width or length, is sturdy, and does not warp indoors. Many lumberyards will cut plywood to whatever size you want, although some make a small charge for this service. Others have scrap pieces of plywood already cut, and you can select from these.

Figure C-2. "Corn," 12 inches by 12 inches. Enamel paints and cut paper on wood.

Figure C-3. "Cherry Tree," 10 inches by 10 inches. Spray enamels on cut wood.

Figure C-4. "Calendulas."

Figure C-5. "Dove," 10 inches by 14 inches. Unpainted weathered wood, with colored felts inserted; white on white felts for background.

Figure C-6. "Hen."

Figure C-7. "Ummm," 10 inches by 12 inches. Stained weathered wood with felt cutouts on felt background.

Figure C-8. "Geese."

Figure C-9. "Where's Adam?" 8 inches by 16 inches. Color stain on weathered wood, with cutouts of wood, paper, and plastic.

Figure C-10. "Village," 10 inches by 12 inches. Enameled woods on walnut stained board.

Figure C-11. "Fish," 10 inches by 10 inches. Enameled wood with paper.

Figure C-12. "Love Bird," 10 inches by 14 inches. Redwood bird on stitched felt backing.

Figure C-13. "Apple," 10 inches by 10 inches. Enameled woods with paper details.

C-2

C-3

C-4

C-5

C-6

C-7

C-8

C-9

C-10

C-11

C-12

C-13

Figure 1-2. "Valentine Bird." Brightly painted wood bird contains a secret which is revealed by lifting the knob. By Ruth Law. (Tom Hurley)

The steps in applying felt to plywood are shown in Figures 1-3 through 1-9. You first measure the felt to allow 2 to 3 inches extra at each edge. Paint the face, or smoothest side of the board, with any household white glue. Pour the glue into a bowl and add water to thin slightly if necessary. A 2-inch brush speeds work and is easy to handle. Cover the surface with a thin layer and do not let the glue puddle. If too much glue is used, it can soak into the felt and spoil its appearance. Once the wood is covered with glue, it should be allowed to dry just slightly. Be sure the board is well coated out to the edges.

If the felt is a light color, you can first place the plywood on the felt, center it, and make a pencil outline around it. Then remove the wood, coat it with glue, and place it with the wet side down on the pencil marks. If the felt is dark, so that pencil marks will not show, crease the felt, or mark the area with pins. When the wood is in place, turn wood and felt upside down so that you can smooth the felt onto the board with your hands. Be sure it is adhered out to the edges. Let it dry face down on a flat surface.

Test in twenty or thirty minutes and when the glue seems dry, paint glue on one of the edges. Fold the felt from the face side over the edge and let the board rest on that edge to dry. Then follow the same procedure on the opposite edge.

When these two edges are dry and smooth, use a razor blade or a scissors to cut away the excess felt at the corners of the glued edges. Then repeat the glueing process for the other two edges. Finally, draw the flaps of felt to the back and miter the corners, cutting away excess material, and glue. Because this work is done in several steps, it may be easier to cover two or three panels at one time. Several days can elapse between steps if that's the way your time works out. It will not matter.

Figure I-3 was cut wood, stained, and placed on a felt background. Lettering, also in felt, was added. Figures C-2 and C-13 (page 19) show other examples of the same combination of wood with felt. Once the panel is felt-covered and thoroughly dry, you have a good solid base panel to which you can easily apply the decorative cutouts. Panels of this kind are sometimes referred to as wood appliqué.

If you plan to apply stained wood rather than an untreated wood to the felt surface, staining must be done first. Put some paint thinner or turpentine into a tuna-fish can and add the coloring paint (enamel or artist's oil color). Stir and then try the stain on a scrap of wood. Once stained, the wood may be made darker by additional layers of stain, or by adding more coloring agent. It cannot be lightened. Use a cloth without lint, such as an old sheet, or a brush, to apply the stain. Let it sit a few minutes; then wipe off the excess. Avoid staining the back side of the wood, as the oil usually prevents the glue from adhering. Place the stained wood on paper to let it dry thoroughly. This process is shown in Figures 1-11 through 1-13.

Figure 1-3. To cover a plywood panel, first cut felt. Allow several extra inches on each edge.

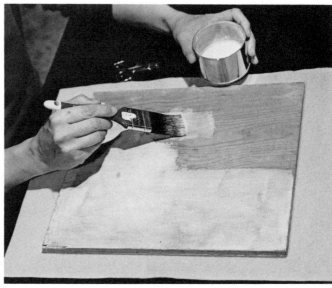

Figure 1-4. Coat best side of the plywood with any white household glue. Thin the glue slightly with water to make it easy to brush on.

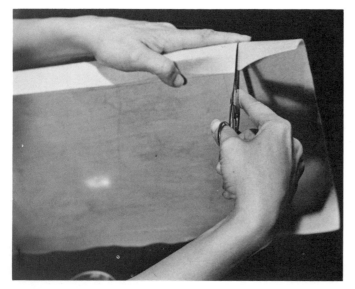

Figure 1-7. Press the felt flat to that edge. Then clip the felt exactly even with the board.

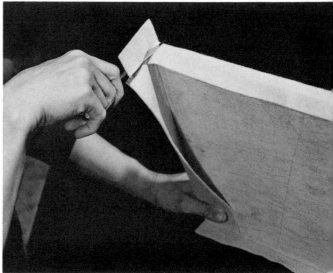

Figure 1-8. Glue a second edge and clip it the same way as the first. This will leave a neat, finished corner which fits perfectly.

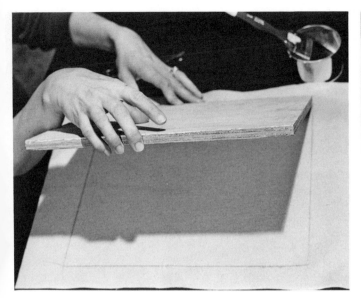

Figure 1-5. Place glued surface of the board face down on felt. A pencil mark will help ensure correct placement. Smooth felt onto the board, using the palms of your hands.

Figure 1-6. After that surface is dry, paint one edge with the glue. Be sure to cover all corners well. Rest it on that edge to dry.

Figure 1-9. When all edges are glued and clipped, cut the excess felt to make a mitered corner which eliminates any overlapping. Glue these cut edges in place.

Place the cut wood pieces on the felt panel to be sure of your arrangement. Then pick up the cut wood pieces, one at a time and apply glue to the back side. Place each back in the desired position on the felt. When all the wood pieces have been glued, lay a book or other flat-surfaced object over them until they are dry. The weight will help to prevent any warping of the wood, which sometimes occurs because of the water-base white glue.

Finally, other colored felts can be cut and added to the background. In doing this, brush the back side of the cut felt pieces lightly with glue. Do not thin the glue for this step, as it is then more likely to soak in. Place the felt pieces carefully! If they are moved, the glue will leave spots on the felt.

"Long-Haired Boy," in Figure 1-10, takes advantage of weathered wood and the natural shape of the board. The width of the board was used for the height of the panel, with the nail holes left to become part of the design. Powdered paint was rubbed on for eyes and cheek.

Another simple panel which incorporates color but avoids painting is "Where's Adam?" Figure C-9 (page 19). A board was cut into two pieces of the same length. The front board was then cut in half to make doors. Inside, a section of wood was cut out and removed, leaving a recessed area. Illustration board or thin plywood was used to back this opening, making it rigid enough so that other cutouts and objects could be attached to it. Hinges were made of grosgrain ribbon and nails. The cut wood was stained with water paint, marking pen, and India ink.

Another example of cutout areas into which new objects can be placed is seen in Figures 1-14 through 1-17. The figure was drawn on wood, and the body was cut in one piece, with arms and legs separate. To cut the open areas, a hole was drilled in the center. The blade of the jigsaw was then inserted through the hole and replaced in the saw. When the interior shape was cut, the blade was removed from the saw so that the figure could slide out. If that seems like too much trouble, or if you don't have a drill, cut in from the outside edge in one line. When the interior shape has been cut, exit through that same line. Or cut the figure in two, putting the parts back together later.

"Pear," Figure I-4, shows an enameled wood cutout on a natural wood ground. A mahogany board was cut to length, and the finished and painted sections of the pear were glued in place. The mahogany piece was not stained or painted, but was oiled lightly. If you have no wood oil, a vegetable cooking oil will do. The oil helps to intensify the grain of the wood. Oil must be applied *last*, or it will prevent the glue from sticking. When glueing a raw board, avoid any smears or oozes from the glue, as it will stain the surface of the wood and show up when the board is oiled.

A 1-inch-thick piece of scrap wood was sawed to make the hand in Figure 1-18. The surface, left rough and unsanded, was painted with latex paint. Lines were painted with acrylic. Then a light spray was used overall.

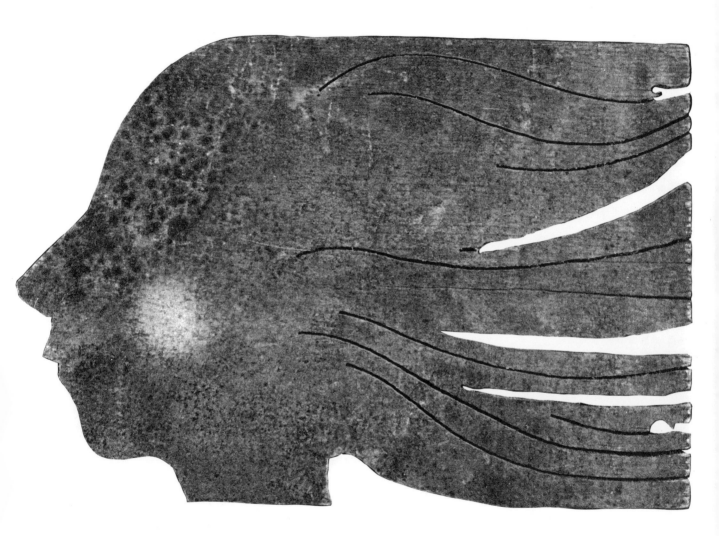

Figure 1-11. To darken cut wood pieces, brush on a thin stain. Be sure to cover all outside edges. Let stain soak in a few minutes. Then wipe the entire surface to remove any excess.

Figure 1-12. Reassemble all pieces and place on the background panel. Coat the back side of each piece with white glue (not thinned) and set it in place.

Figure 1-13. Finally, add cut felt pieces to the background.

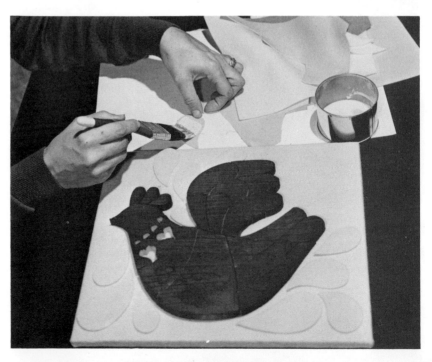

Figure 1-14. Sketch for a figure is first made on wood with a marking pen. When space ran short here, the legs were drawn on another section of wood giving a change in grain direction.

Figure 1-15. The center is removed in one piece by making a cut in from the bottom. Figure is then assembled.

Figure 1-16. Small forms are cut from thinner wood to be used as insets.

Figure 1-17. When final arrangement is determined, all small cut pieces and parts of figure are glued to a background panel. Finished piece is 7 inches by 20 inches.

Figure 1-18. "That Way," 8 inches. The pointing hand is cut from a scrap wood board painted with latex paint. Lines are added with acrylic.

Figure 1-19. Simple screen, 13 inches by 18 inches, is made from hinged boards embellished with paint, tissue paper, Mother Goose cutouts, and stain.

Another quick method of treating wood is to apply a colored paper. In the small screen shown in Figure 1-19, tissue papers were used to add the main areas of color. The 6-inch-wide board was cut into three pieces, and each was arched at the top. Very little sawing is required if you start with a board of the right width. When you work with scrap wood, it is often easier to adjust your design to the available material. The arches were painted with white latex. Then the colored tissue paper was added. The tissue was cut into arch shapes smaller than the wood. White glue was applied to the surface of the wood and the tissue placed on top of that. As it is almost impossible to keep tissue paper perfectly smooth, plan to wrinkle it. This adds an interesting texture and pattern which is emphasized later on when you stain over the paper. When the tissue was dry, cutouts from an old Mother Goose book were glued onto it. Finally, a stain was wiped over the entire surface to darken and emphasize the wrinkles. This also blends, or unifies, the latex background, tissue, and colored cutouts. Two pairs of small hinges were used to join the panels. Or a simple hinge can be made with fabric by glueing the fabric on in the same way that a metal hinge would be attached. A carpet tack driven through fabric and wood will make it stronger. See Figure 1-24.

Figure 1-20. "Flower," 6 inches high. It is cut from pine and painted white. Color is added through the layering of tissue papers and stains.

Figure 1-21. "Bird." Bright tissue paper cutouts are applied to the white form to add color.

32

Figure 1-22. "Peace Dove," 9 inches square. Details cut from coated paper add an opaque color to the painted surface.

Figure 1-23. "Fish," 9 inches long. It is composed of cut and painted wood. The "textured" background is the unintentional result of combining incompatible paints — in this case, lacquer over enamel.

The flower and bird in Figures 1-20 and 1-21 show other uses of tissue over latex-covered wood. Undercoat, or gesso, may be used in place of latex. The flower shape was cut from ½-inch-thick pine, painted, and then tissue paper cutouts were applied over white glue. When dry, a stain was rubbed over it. The stain was deliberately left heavier in some areas than in others. The bird project used the same procedure. A finishing coat of clear shellac, lacquer, or plastic varnish can then be added. Use whatever you have at hand.

Tissue can also be applied by sticking it directly to a pre-painted board that has been coated with shellac, lacquer, or plastic. Paint on a coat of clear finish, place tissue on this while it is still wet, and then add another layer of finish. This method gives a bright, shiny look that makes the colors of the tissue paper very brilliant. It also gives a finished surface, although stain cannot be applied as easily over this smooth finish. If left in sunlight, the color of tissue paper will eventually fade. Since this way of working is especially easy and speedy, and it takes so little time to do a new panel, you should not be concerned about the fading.

Another means of decorating the finished painted wood is by adding small pieces of cut paper. I find Color-Aid to be the most satisfactory. It is a clay-coated paper, fairly stiff, and one that does not curl easily when glued. It comes in a beautiful range of colors, but be careful in handling it, because it shows fingerprints readily. When the paper pieces have been cut, and the arrangement determined, a white glue is used on the back. Press the paper in place, being sure it is flat against the wood. Avoid being generous or messy with the glue, but if you are, wipe away any excess glue with a damp cloth. When the paper work is finished and dry, the paper should be coated with a plastic finish or fixative. In Figure 1-22, the details on the bird are paper, as are some of the leaves and berries.

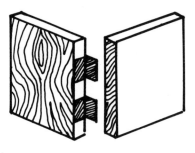

Figure 1-24. A simple hinge can be made by glueing fabric or ribbon to wood edges that are to be hinged.

Be sure to read labels on the paints and finishes you use, checking to see which ones are compatible. The "Fish" in Figure 1-23 has an unintentionally textured background, which resulted from spraying lacquer over enamel. The enamel crawled. The "Fish" also shows the use of cut colored papers applied to wood. A paper punch was used to cut out the many small circles.

In sawing designs from wood, the large simple shapes are always cut first; the smaller, more intricate shapes next, and the fine details last. Design so that your first shape, or first cut, is just an outline. Then elaborate by dividing the first shape into smaller portions. Finally, make small inside cuts. Figures 1-25, 1-26, 1-27, and 1-28 show how to simplify for initial cuts, and how to get more complex as you progress.

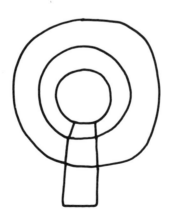

Figure 1-25. To simplify the sawing of the hen, first cut just the head and the body piece. Then go back and cut the tail, comb, and bill. The large area is then cut into four smaller ones. Each of these begins to take on pattern as they are cut into even smaller shapes.

Figure 1-26. The simple outline cut is made first. Then the trunk and smaller circles are cut. By the time you get to the petal shapes, they are just half-circles cut at the edge.

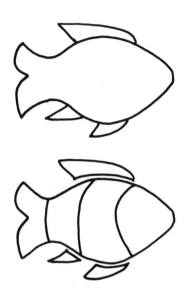

Figure 1-27. The fish shape is cut first; then the fins. Again each area is broken up into smaller ones.

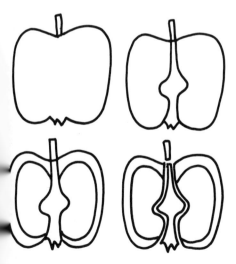

Figure 1-28. By cutting around the apple, all cuts are easy to do. The stem is made separately. The lines through the center, around the seeds, open up the inside so that even the enclosed shapes are simply done.

Figure 1-29. "Mother," 14 inches high. Made of acrylic modeling paste on plywood, with acrylic paints. It is one of a series based on old tattoo and advertising art. By Bruce Butte.

2. Architectural Panels

Wood appliqué is easily adapted to large-scale work. If you have managed a small wood project, then you can also work at an architectural scale. This usually involves relating the work in some way to the structural elements of a room or an area. Sometimes size alone does this. At other times, panels may go from floor to ceiling, be aligned with structural members or beams, or stretch over an entire wall.

The primary difference in working large scale is that there is simply more of it. If you have produced one square

wood panel, then you only need more panels to cover a larger wall or door. A unit design can be repeated to cover a larger area. If the wall is to be one composition (that is, one single design, not a repeat unit), then the composition will be more difficult. To simplify design on a first project, work with a composite, or collection, using a module, or repeated shape. You need not do a whole wall. A floor-to-ceiling vertical section, or panel, may enhance a room more successfully.

2-1. "Hand," unfinished weathered wood, is about a three-minute project.

If you have 10-inch boards, use the 10-inch width as the unit size and cut squares. These can serve as the backgrounds for appliqué wood panels. See Figure 2-2 as an example of grouping these small panels. An advantage in this approach is that you do not need special materials or large pieces of wood — just more of the small ones. Chapter 4 has further examples of the use of small units used in repeat to cover large areas.

I prefer to draw my designs directly on the wood, but you may draw them on paper first if you like. Follow the procedure shown in Figures 2-3 through 2-12. The paper pattern is drawn first and cut. It is then traced onto a piece of ½-inch pine. Saw the big simple shapes first. Then go back to cut some of the larger shapes into smaller ones. When all the cuts have been made, reassemble the parts. Then sand, paint the top and sides only with undercoat, and sand again lightly. Use a medium sandpaper for the first sanding and a fine one on the dry undercoat.

Figure 2-2. "Foods Panels," in cut and painted wood, from ½-inch pine. Each panel is 12 inches by 56 inches. By Joyce Aiken and Jean Ray Laury.

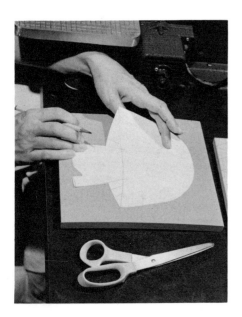

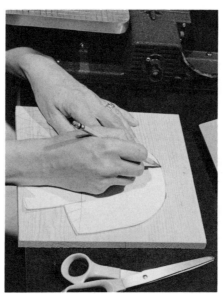

Figure 2-3. Paper pattern from drawing may be placed on the finished background panel to be sure of size and placement.

Figure 2-4. Next place the paper pattern on the unfinished wood from which the design is to be sawed. Draw lightly around the paper pattern with a soft lead pencil.

Figure 2-5. After the outline of the main shape is drawn, add any other shapes to the same board. Place them to make best use of the wood, but allow enough space to cut between them. Cut the large simple shapes first, moving the wood slowly through the saw.

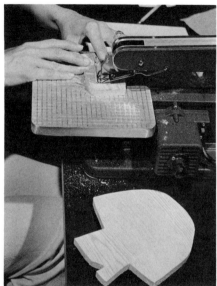

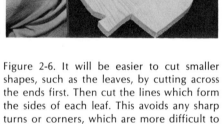

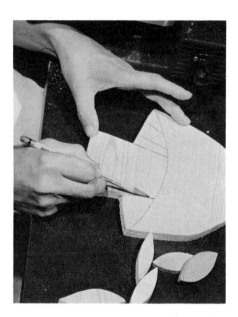

Figure 2-6. It will be easier to cut smaller shapes, such as the leaves, by cutting across the ends first. Then cut the lines which form the sides of each leaf. This avoids any sharp turns or corners, which are more difficult to do.

Figure 2-7. After the large shapes have been cut, go back and sketch in the smaller divisions.

Figure 2-8. Cut from the largest shapes to the smallest. Put the sawed pieces back into place as you cut them, or you may find the jigsaw pieces difficult to reassemble.

 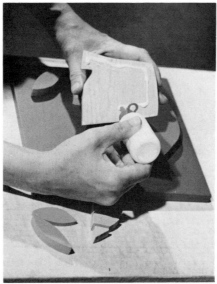 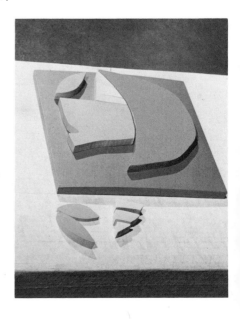

Figure 2-9. When sawing is finished, the cut edges must be sanded. Use a medium-to-fine sandpaper, and remove all burrs, or rough spots. Use a fine sandpaper on the surface of the wood if necessary. After sanding, wipe all the cut wood with a slightly damp cloth. This will remove all dust before the undercoating is applied. The layer of undercoat may be applied from a spray can or by brush. Be sure to cover the edges of each piece well, but avoid too heavy a coat that will run or drip. When undercoat is dry, another light sanding may be needed.

Figure 2-10. Wipe wood again before starting to paint. If the wood is not completely free of dust and particles, it will not have a smooth surface. Paint may be applied from a spray can or by brush. When paint is dry, use white glue to attach painted wood pieces to the backing panel.

Figure 2-11. Be sure placement is correct, since removing the glued pieces will damage the background.

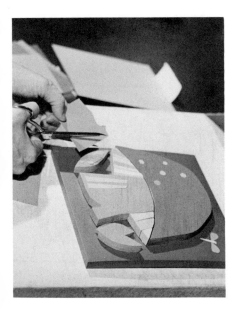

Figure 2-12. Final step is the addition of cut paper pieces. The back side of the paper pieces must be completely coated with white glue. Then place them carefully on the wood. Wipe away any excess glue. If any glue smears, use a damp cloth to clean that area. When all papers are glued in place and cleaned, the paper may be brushed with a plastic finish.

Figure 2-13. The finished panel was made from the preceding steps.

Figure 2-15. "Kitchen Panel" (detail). Spaghetti, lentils, and seeds are added to the fabrics and papers in this wood appliqué panel.

Figure 2-14. "Lemons." Wood panel. By Joyce Aiken.

Figure 2-16. "Kitchen Panel," 24 inches by 6 feet, 8 inches. it was commissioned by the Robert Beechings, Fresno, for use in a kitchen-dining area. By Jean Ray Laury.

Figure 2-17. "Ladies in the Spring," 24 inches by 44 inches. A white-on-white painted wood panel. By Joyce Aiken.

Figure 2-18. "Wood Panel," 40 inches by 48 inches. Rare hard woods are sanded and sealed to leave a rich natural finish. It was commissioned by Mr. and Mrs. Eugene C. Reid, Bakersfield, California. By Patricia Hopper.

Figure 2-19. "Wood Panel" (detail). This shows how the saw has been used as a drawing tool to divide large areas into smaller ones and to add a linear pattern.

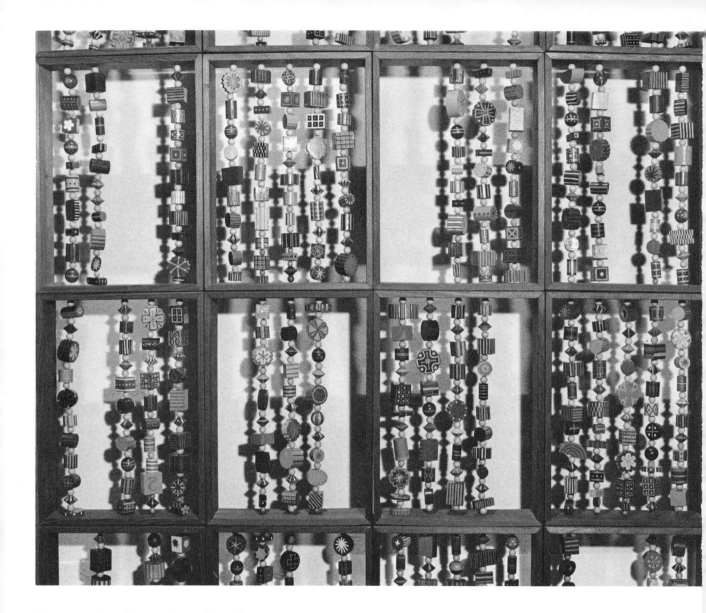

Figure 2-20. "Wood Screen," 40 inches wide.
It has a delightful pattern of color and shapes.
By Ruth Law.

Small pieces of wood, such as those shown in the step-by-step process, can be glued to a backing with a household white glue. Paint a thin layer of the glue (or squeeze a light line) onto the back side of the cut wood pieces. Then place them on the panel. Put a few books on top of them to avoid any warping while they dry. Be careful that small pieces of wood do not slip or slide out of position.

To produce a large panel where the wood squares must be attached to a backing panel, white glue is not always satisfactory. Warping may be a problem, as the white glue has a water base and is absorbed by the raw wood. Use either a wood glue or epoxy.

The "Kitchen Panel" in Figure 2-16, commissioned for a dining-room, is a combination of natural, stained, and painted wood. Some ready-made objects were used, such as spoons and a cutting board. Peppercorns, coffee beans, and various seeds and spices also added details and textural contrast to shiny-smooth enamel areas. These are easily seen in the detail in Figure 2-15. Patterned fabrics are glued to wood with white glue, as are wood tapes and colored papers.

"Ladies in the Spring," Figure 2-13 is a white-on-white panel which capitalizes on the relief pattern of wood for its design. Since the cut wood pieces and background are all painted the same color, only the shadows tend to separate them. The overlapping, or projecting, wood piece lets the "Lady" break out of the confines of the panel. Masonite was cut for many of the shapes used. It comes in very thin sheets, and it gives a variation in thickness, adding another dimension of interest to the panel.

Masonite has a nice smooth surface and rarely needs any sanding except for the edges. Be sure to use tempered Masonite, which has a hard surface. The untempered kind is very porous and will simply swallow the paint without giving you a smooth painted surface. Masonite comes with one side smooth and one side scored, or with two sides smooth. Either will do, although if both sides are smooth, the Masonite will lie flatter on the panel. Another advantage to using Masonite is that it is available in large sheets, rather than in board form, so that very large shapes can be cut in a single piece. Scrap pieces of Masonite are often available at lumberyards, and are sold by the square foot. It really works best to combine Masonite with other, thicker woods. Small circles are more easily cut from Masonite than from thicker wood, but the simplest way to cut circles is to slice a large dowel. Some woodworkers, carried away by their adventures in wood, have been known to saw up the handles of their brooms and dust mops. These offer a good-sized dowel for circles. A broken rake handle will do as well. Or you can use an old closet pole.

The large wood panel in Figure 2-18 depicts the flora and fauna native to the area where the work was to be installed. By using all natural wood colors, a beautiful range from the off-whites and honey-colored woods to the rich reds and deep browns was achieved. The surfaces have been polished smooth and oiled. Oiling intensifies color and allows the grain of the wood to become an important element in the design. This panel is also shown in Figure C-29 (page 56).

Some of the animal forms are separated from the background with additional pieces of wood so that they tend to float out from the backing. In other areas, the animal is cut out from the background so that it appears in reverse, or negative. The result is a glowing and richly ornamented surface.

The room divider, or wood screen, in Figure 2-20 is made up of small painted handmade beads. Dowels of various widths, square wood strips, and wooden curtain rods were cut into various lengths and drilled through the centers.

The dowels were sliced to make beads which are horizontal as well as vertical. It is probably easier to paint these by hand, since it is difficult with a spray can to cover evenly an uneven surface. When sprayed, one section tends to drip with paint while another remains uncoated. By placing the beads on toothpicks or tiny wood skewers, they can be dried without having the wet paint touch any other surface. The toothpicks can be held upright by inserting them into a chunk of Plasticine or clay, or, if you have neither, a styrofoam chunk or a potato.

The size of your work with wood cutting and painting need not be limited by tools or materials. If you wish to work on an architectural scale, it will just require more time, more energy, and a little more imagination. Many large-scale projects, particularly in your own home, can be done in sections or parts. As the parts are completed, they can be hung or installed so that the work can be enjoyed as it progresses.

Figure C-14. "Foods Panels," 36 inches by 76 inches. Painted wood designs are applied to painted 10-inch squares. The finished squares are then attached to a large panel of ½-inch plywood, enameled white. The frame is redwood. Commissioned for Student Union lunchroom at Fresno State University. By Joyce Aiken and Jean Ray Laury.

Figure C-15. Beaded screen in sections 9 inches by 12 inches. Beads are made of cut dowels, wood scraps, commercial wood beads, and sliced wood curtain rods. Each bead is hand-painted, decorated, and strung into a frame. By Ruth Law.

Figure C-16. "Kitchen Panel" (detail), 24 inches high. Paper and fabric are used to decorate the wood cutouts. Various kitchen articles, such as mixing spoons, scoop, spaghetti, and rolling pin are also included. By Jean Ray Laury.

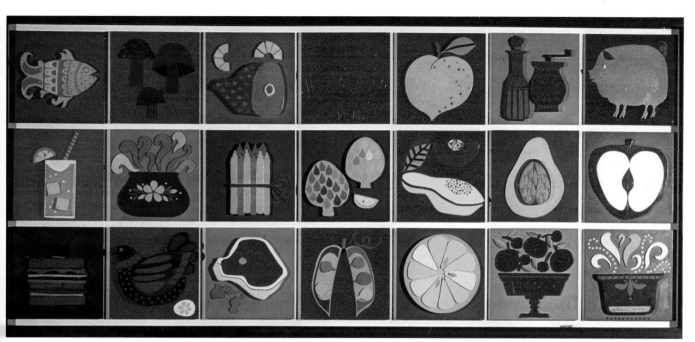

C-14

C-15   C-16

3. Ready-Made Objects

Figure 3-1. "Star." Wood painted with acrylic. 4 inches. By Lizabeth Laury. (Tom Hurley)

Unpainted, unfinished, or just plain old wood furniture offers a great beginning for your wood painting. The use of ready-made objects and boxes endlessly expands the possibilities of working with wood. These projects allow you to enjoy the decorative aspects of cutting and painting wood without becoming involved in construction. The craftsman possessing only a paint brush can enjoy this decorative fantasy without access to even a minimum shop or tools.

Once you start looking, you will find ready-made things everywhere. These can be painted only, or they can be embellished with painted wood cutouts. The salt and pepper shakers shown in Figure C-31 (page 73) were purchased in a department store. They come in natural wood, or in color, and can be sanded before repainting. For the best surface, an additional coat of undercoat should be added and then the enamel color. An easy way to divide the surface into areas of color is simply to use the divisions, or sections, already suggested by the pattern of the turning. Then you can go back and

paint details to whatever extent you are able. A fine-pointed sable brush will be of great value in doing this work.

Wood boxes may also be decorated with wood cutouts in which only stains are used. Figure 3-3 shows such a box. By using an assortment of woods, the colors can vary from white birch to dark walnut, and a finishing coat is all that is needed. Or the designs may be cut from one piece of wood, with a variety of stains used on the different sections.

The common cigar box was once readily available with its richly ornamented paper medallions and gold paint. You may still be fortunate enough to locate one if you ask at your local tobacco store. To take advantage of the profusion of color and design which usually adorns these boxes, wood may be applied over the paper, giving a patterned background. The paper can be partially sanded away and then stained or it can be removed entirely by soaking with a damp sponge. Use just enough water to loosen the paper without warping the wood.

Figure 3-4 shows a small wood box, enameled, with an overall decorative design. Another painted wood box is shown in Figure 3-5. Quarter-inch-thick wood veneer was used for the cutouts shown in Figure 3-6. The veneer is easily sawed because it is thin and it is a nice wood to work with.

Wood recipe boxes, or wood card-file boxes, offer good smooth areas for wood cutouts. A walk through any import shop or ten-cent store will turn up a variety of wood objects for decoration. Spools, butter paddles, scrub brushes, spoons, and trays are but a few. Wood spoons have inviting surfaces for decoration. Even a wood comb or a shoehorn can be transformed from a very ordinary object to a very special one with some decorative painting.

Old wood chairs give you a great opportunity for detailed decorative painting. The knobbier the better, as knobs and divisions on legs and backs make the designing and painting simpler. The high chair in Figure C-30 (page 73) is enameled so that each separate piece of the chair, or plane of the wood, is a color change. The kitchen chair has carefully painted details over the impressed design on the chair back. See Figure C-32 (page 73).

An unfinished wood headboard makes a good base for wood appliqué. By selecting boards of an easily used width (about 6 inches or 8 inches for a twin, or double-size, headboard), the board itself can become part of the design. If your resources for sawing are limited to a jigsaw or a coping saw, it will help to have these boards cut to the correct length at the lumberyard. See Figure 3-8 on how to plan this. Figures 3-9 and 3-10 suggest a way of utilizing the board width as part of the design.

You will also find it helpful to use a positive-negative approach to the design. See Figure 3-11. This simply means that you must saw carefully so that both the background and the foreground pieces can be used. The shape you saw out, as well as the background shape left over, become parts of the design. This serves several purposes. It unifies the design by repeating shapes; it conserves your energy in sawing; and it makes the fullest possible use of the wood. Figures 3-12 and 3-13 suggest some possibilities of this technique. Figures C-40 and C-41 show other headboards which use this technique of integrating positive and negative shapes. The trains in Figures C-37 and C-45 (page 73) are wood appliqués designed as headboards for children's beds.

Use either an old headboard which you may already have and can refinish, or buy an unfinished wood one to paint. Consider the possibility that the rectangular headboard panel can be hung separately on the wall above the head of a bed without actually being attached to the bed frame. It is best to paint and to finish the blank headboard completely first, and then to start adding the cut and painted wood pieces. All parts should have their final coats of paint before they are glued in place.

Figure 3-2. Painted Wood Cylinder Box, 4 inches. By Ruth Law. (Stan Bitters)

C-17

C-18

C-19

C-20

C-21

C-22

C-23

C-24

C-25

C-26

C-27

C-28

C-29

A chest of drawers offers several nice flat areas for decoration. Figure C-34 (page 73) shows one which also appears in the closeup in Figure 3-16. In this one, a thin wood veneer called wood tape was used for the appliqué. This veneer comes in a strip, a roll, or a sheet, and can be purchased in different wood finishes. It can easily be cut with a scissors, X-acto knife, or a single-edge razor blade. In the illustration, the stems, leaves, and berries were cut and glued to the flat surface of the drawer front. Take the drawer out of the chest and stand it on its back to make the work easier. After all glueing was finished and each piece was securely in place, everything was painted over with a colored latex paint. When dry, a stain, or antiqueing glaze, was rubbed over the top to darken depressions. Some stain is deliberately allowed to catch in corners to emphasize the design.

Another chest, in Figure C-42 (page 73) shows solid-colored drawer fronts in various related hues. Decorative painting is limited to the flat knobs.

The candleholder, Figure C-38 (page 73), was assembled from blocks of wood, stacked with additional wood pieces glued on the sides of some of the blocks. Beveled edges and wood moldings, often available from lumberyards or paint stores, are a simple way to add much more detail. If you are assembling the candleholder yourself, it will be much easier to paint the individual parts before joining them.

Candleholders cut from old table legs can be decoratively painted, and the more ornate the better. If they are at all unstable, glue each candleholder to a solid chunk of wood or a board as a base.

If decorative painting is new to you, choose the simplest kind of design to begin with. To help with spacing or placement, use a pin prick or a pencil dot to guide yourself. You may make a guide with paint, too. For example, to paint a random bunch of flowers, first paint a dot for the center of each. Put one line through the dot. Then cross it at right angles to make a plus sign. After that, you need only divide the open areas in half. See Figure 3-14. Use a ruler if you feel safer, but remember that some variations and differences will inevitably give an individual and more personal look to the piece. If you are painting by hand, do not strive to make it look machine printed. Avoid hard lines and geometric shapes since they will be the most difficult to keep looking smooth and continuous.

Figure 3-3. Ready-Made Box, 5 inches by 8½ inches. Stained wood appliqué. By Marlo Johansen.

Figure 3-4. Ready-Made Box, 3 inches by 4 inches. Painted wood cutout appliqué. By Ruth Law.

Figure 3-5. Painted Box. The pattern used on the side of the box is repeated on the lid in bright enamels. 4 inches high. By Ruth Law.

Figure 3-6. Wood Box, 3 inches by 8 inches. Simple shapes cut from a thin sheet of birch retain the natural color and wood grain for pattern. By Jean Ray Laury.

Figure 3-7. Headboard. Detail of Flower Garden, using repeated designs in a positive-negative pattern. By Joyce Aiken and Jean Ray Laury.

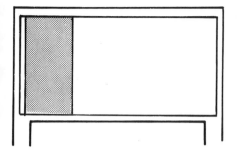

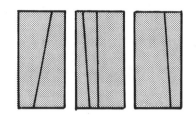

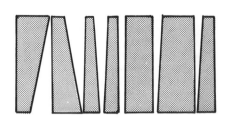

Figure 3-8. Have your wood cut to the length that will fit into the headboard. Clear pine is a good wood to use if you are going to paint it, and it comes in many widths.

Figure 3-9. The cut boards can be sawed into angles that make use of the ready-cut edges.

Figure 3-10. The sawed boards can then be reassembled into a pattern.

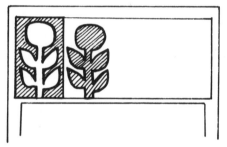

Figure 3-11. By cutting carefully, the inside shape can be kept intact and removed. Cut the large shape first; then the details. The result is a positive-negative pattern which conserves time, energy, and wood, as well as adds a repeat element to the design.

Figure 3-12. The repeated design works back and forth. Cut the flower and stem first. Then go back and cut the leaves separately.

Figure 3-13. The same approach to design can be used with a variety of board widths. In each cut, the positive and negative shapes are used.

Figure 3-14. Any flower, star, or circular pattern will be easier to paint if you start with a dot for the center.

Figure 3-15. Chest. Drawer fronts only are treated with wood veneer cutouts appliquéd to the wood surface. Chest is 30 inches high. By Jean Ray Laury.

Figure 3-16. Chest (detail). After painting the entire chest, a stain was applied over the glued-on cutouts. The stain emphasized the cut edges as well as the grain of the veneer.

4. Doors

Figure 4-1. Double doors for residence. Enameled wood appliqué. Each door is 30 inches by 80 inches. By Jean Ray Laury.

Doors provide more than a means for entering or leaving a room or a house. They also provide a mood. They suggest an inviting entry, or a forbidding passageway. The door can be friendly or austere, intimate or anonymous. It can be warm in color and alive with pattern, or as cold as steel bars.

Doors carry great symbolic overtones. Our language is full of expressions relating to open doors, closed doors, and thresholds, and all suggest the symbolic values we attribute to them. So whether it is imposing or humble, nondescript or sensational, the door does make an initial statement. It has an impact on the person who approaches it.

Most houses today have standard, unembellished doors. They are like big blank canvases or sheets of drawing paper, waiting for someone to bring them to life. A decorative door can make the mere act of passing through it a delightful experience. Being somewhat related in scale to human beings, doors have always offered a means of personalizing access to a house or a room. An impersonal one may seem forbidding because it offers no clues as to what lies inside — being neither friendly nor hostile. A door opens to allow entry, but it can also be a means of shutting persons out.

The most direct means of letting a door "speak" is a very common one. The eight-year-old who puts a huge skull and crossbones, with "Keep Out," on his door makes his message clear. Even if it amuses his mother, his sister knows that access is restricted! The boy's father may accomplish the same thing at his office with "Private Entrance," or "Authorized Personnel Only." Doors that read "Come In," or "Enter," also communicate — but it is easy and fun to go beyond this absolute minimum. A welcome sign need not always be relegated to the doormat. The door can say welcome as well. It commits you to your word, of course. The doormat can be whipped out of sight on a bad day when you do not want visitors, while it's more difficult to remove your door. But there are substitutes for words. You can welcome guests with bright color, rich subdued color, abstract patterns, or a profusion of flowers.

Whether you wish to do a door for inside or outside, the simplest approach is to use a door that is already installed. Remove the hinge pins so that you can place the wood surface flat while you work on it. If the door is panelled with raised and recessed areas, take advantage of the level changes. Part of your work is already done for you. The first consideration should probably be given to the use of the door — whether it is a front door, a garage door, to a storage room, bathroom, child's room, or basement. The use of the room may suggest an appropriate design or color.

Don't be afraid of your door. It is not a sacred object, and it can easily be repaired or replaced if your results should actually be disastrous. If you would feel more comfortable, measure an inside door (where airtight fitting is not so essential). Then check a lumberyard or a builder's salvage company for a used door of the same size. When you have finished making it glorious, exchange the doors. You can continue this kind of a doorway musical chairs throughout the house, always having one extra door on which to work.

Figure 4-2. The Spanish-style architecture of the restaurant suggested use of the arch form. Arches vary in size and color and use both the positive and negative shapes of each cut. Each door is 32 inches by 80 inches. By Jean Ray Laury.

Figure 4-3. Board to be decorated is first painted with latex or gesso. The color can be added by staining, or by glueing colored tissue to the wood. Here the excess tissue is cut away from the edge after the glue has dried.

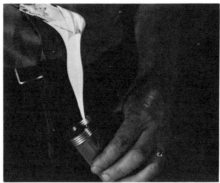

Figure 4-4. Acrylic spackle should be about the consistency of 7-minute frosting. Thin spackle slightly with water if necessary. The tube is filled with thinned spackle. Be sure the nozzle end is in place. Use a plain, round nozzle opening rather than a decorative, or star-shaped, opening.

Figure 4-5. Plunger is set in place to force spackle down and to avoid air bubbles.

Figures 4-8 and 4-9. Largest shapes are always made first. Then work down to the smaller ones. In this series, a daisy form is varied to fit the different rectangular shapes.

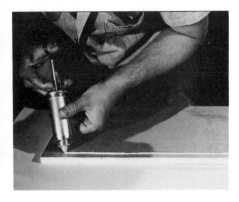

Figure 4-6. The edge of the nozzle can be placed at an angle against the wood for support. The spackle drawing may be done freehand, or a light pencil drawing can be done on the wood.

Figure 4-7. A way of simplifying the design is to divide the large rectangles into smaller ones. These smaller shapes can then be treated individually with circles and squiggles.

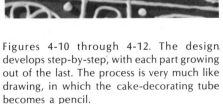

Figures 4-10 through 4-12. The design develops step-by-step, with each part growing out of the last. The process is very much like drawing, in which the cake-decorating tube becomes a pencil.

Figures 4-13 through 4-15. A full view of the panel shows the way spaces are divided and filled in for an overall pattern that is very detailed and decorative.

Figures 4-16 and 4-17. These two panels represent other examples of the decorative-spackle method. Illustration boards were painted and glued to the backing wood. These provided space divisions in the largest area. Then the designs filled these individual spaces.

Figure 4-18. Sanded and sealed hardwood gives a satin smooth finish to the sun in this panel from a door, 11 inches wide. By Patricia Hopper.

Figure 4-19. Door (detail). The natural darks and lights of the walnut were utilized in the intricately cut suns. By Patricia Hopper.

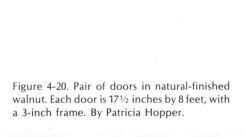

Figure 4-20. Pair of doors in natural-finished walnut. Each door is 17½ inches by 8 feet, with a 3-inch frame. By Patricia Hopper.

For a child's room, some of his own drawings might be cut out of wood and appliquéd. Animal or people cutouts placed on a horizontal panel make a good door design. After a few years, when the child outgrows the drawings, the boards can be removed without damaging the cutouts, or the door. See Figure 4-23 for some possible ways of doing this.

Figure C-49 (page 76) shows a cut, painted, and appliquéd wood door commissioned for a conference room. Hardwood was used for durability. All wood pieces were first cut to size and sanded to a smooth finish. Then a layer of undercoat was painted on, followed by another light sanding. Some of the pieces required a second undercoat, though most did not. Colors were added by spray painting. To do this, a plastic tent was built in my backyard to prevent spray from completely covering the azaleas as well as the wood, and to keep insects off the wet paint. It is not ordinarily necessary to take so much precaution, but there were four doors to be painted, each on both sides. That made a total of eight panels, 2½ feet by 9 feet — which is a lot of painting! Be sure to do any spray painting out-of-doors, or in a well-ventilated porch or basement.

When the wood pieces were finished, they were placed in the arrangements shown on the door. Epoxy cement was used to attach the woods to one another, though one or two of the smallest pieces of wood in each panel were not epoxied. When everything else was cemented, these small loose pieces were removed. This made it possible to drill through all layers into the door itself. Wood screws were used to join all layers, and the small cut pieces were then glued back over the top to cover the heads of the countersunk screws. This procedure is not necessary on a door to be used in your own home. Since the door described was in a public building, both the use of hardwoods and wood screws seemed advisable. The solid wood doors were 1½ inches thick to start with. By the time both sides were covered with the appliquéd wood pieces, some areas were 8 inches thick.

Figure C-30. Old High Chair. Refinished and painted. By Ruth Law.

Figure C-31. Manufactured salt and pepper shakers of wood are treated with intricate enameled details.10 inches high. By Ruth Law.

Figures C-32 and C-33. Rocking Chair. Color changes on the chair were suggested by the decorative shapes of the wood turning. By Ruth Law.

Figure C-34. Chest. Shapes cut from wood veneer are glued in place on the surface of the chest. Then the entire area is painted and stained. By Jean Ray Laury.

Figure C-35. Painted Wood Spoons.

Figure C-36. Wheel from gypsy cart. Hand-painted details from Fresno Storyland, designed by Patricia Hopper.

Figure C-37. Child's Headboard (detail). Pine, masonite, and wood veneer are used in the appliqué of train, passengers, and hillside. By Joyce Aiken and Jean Ray Laury.

Figure C-38. Candleholder, 45 inches high. Cut wood pieces are assembled and painted. By Gordon Brofft and Ruth Law.

Figure C-39. Box. Quarter-inch wood veneer was appliquéd to the natural wood surface of a ready-made box. By Jean Ray Laury.

Figure C-40 and C-41. King-size Headboards, with appliquéd wood designs. By Joyce Aiken and Jean Ray Laury.

Figure C-42. Chest, simply painted, with each drawer a different color. Decorative details are used on the drawer pulls only. By Ruth Law.

Figure C-43. Commercially made wood box with enamel painting. By Ruth Law.

Figures C-44 and C-45. Headboards, twin size, in painted wood appliqué. By Joyce Aiken and Jean Ray Laury.

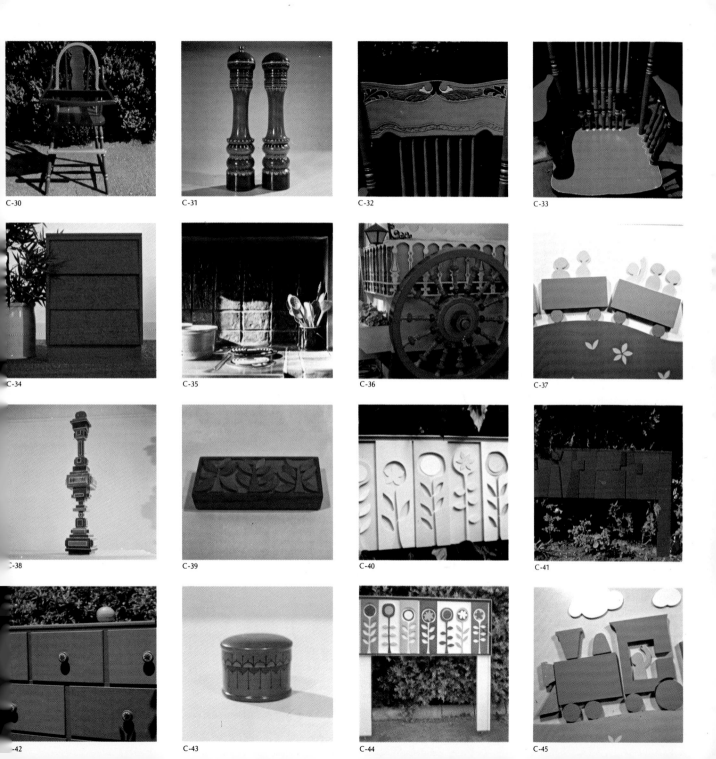

C-30

C-31

C-32

C-33

C-34

C-35

C-36

C-37

C-38

C-39

C-40

C-41

-42

C-43

C-44

C-45

The doors shown in Figure 4-1 were made from white pine. Epoxy was used to attach wood, but no wood screws. Picture-frame molding divided the doors into smaller sections.

By selecting wood of the desired finished width, much of your cutting is already done for you. This makes very efficient use of your materials and keeps cutting to a minimum. Figure 4-24 illustrates this.

In Figure 4-2, another example of minimized cutting is seen. When shapes are cut, both the positive and negative forms are utilized. In these doors, commissioned for a restaurant, the design related to the arches of the Spanish-style architecture. See Figure C-46 (page 76). The arches are repeated over and over, in variations of size and color. Figure 4-25 shows how these were cut and then assembled.

In making your own door, try first to divide the door into sections, or smaller areas. You will find it much easier to work on these smaller areas, and the total project will not seem quite so overwhelming. If your door is not paneled, you might use horizontal boards or a series of squares or verticals. See Figures 4-26 and 4-27, which suggest some possible arrangements.

Figure 4-21. Simple wood cutout, 4 inches. Made at age five by Lizabeth Laury. (Tom Hurley)

Following page:

Figure C-46. Pair of doors in wood appliqué, 64 inches by 80 inches. Commissioned for a restaurant in Canoga Park, California. By Jean Ray Laury. (Frank B. Laury)

Figure C-47. Double doors made from walnut. Each door is 17½ inches by 8 feet. A natural finish is used on the many faces of the sun. Framed in walnut. By Patricia Hopper.

Figure C-48. Interior set of double doors, 5 feet by 9 feet. Hardwood, spray painted in brilliant enamels. Commissioned for the Student Union at Fresno State University, California. By Jean Ray Laury. (Micha Langer)

Figure C-49. Wood appliqué and picture frame molding was used in doors for a residence; 60 inches by 80 inches. By Jean Ray Laury. (Frank B. Laury)

Figure C-50. Acrylic spackle, squeezed through a cake-decorating tube, was used to add the detail to painted panels for a door 30 inches by 80 inches. By Stan Bitters.

Figure C-51. Exterior set of double doors, 5 feet by 9 feet. Hardwood was spray-painted. Commissioned for entrance to the Safstrom Memorial Room, Student Union, Fresno State University, California. By Jean Ray Laury. (Micha Langer)

Figure 4-22. "Animals," 4 inches to 6 inches. Made at age six by Lizabeth Laury. (Tom Hurley)

C-46

C-47

C-48

C-49

C-50

C-51

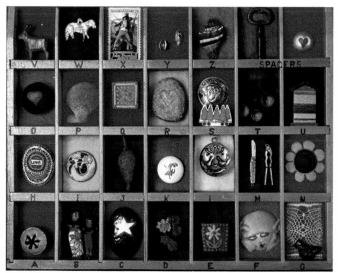

C-52

C-54

Figure C-52. Small Type-case, 8½ inches by 10½ inches. Sections are filled with fabrics, felts, and papers to give an overall patchwork background. Small collector's items are attached inside the sections.

Figure C-53. Soft-Drink Box, 12 inches by 18 inches, stained dark, provides ready-made cubicles for a collection of figures and faces.

Figure C-54. Type-Setter's Large Case Drawer, 17 inches by 32 inches. A collection of thimbles, hands, toys, and small handmade articles are housed in the shallow boxes.

Three boxes by Jean Ray Laury.

C-53

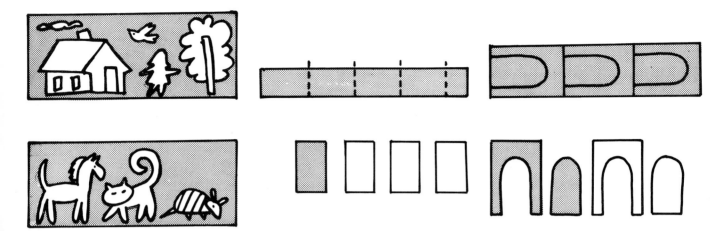

Figure 4-23. Children's drawings can be transferred to wood, or let the children draw directly on the wood. When shapes are sawed and painted, glue them to a board that fits into the door molding, or makes a horizontal band across the door.

Figure 4-24. To cut rectangles, buy wood of the same width that you want in your finished rectangle. That way, over half of your cutting is already done.

Figure 4-25. If arch shapes are cut carefully from the background, both the positive and negative shapes can be used. This saves wood, energy, and sawing time.

Figure 4-26 and 27. Small wood cutouts, glued to larger panels, make a good overall door design. These can be used as horizontal panels, or as a series of rectangles.

Another possibility for a decorative door is shown in Figure C-50 (page 76). In this, illustration board, or similar hard cardboard, was cut and glued to the door to divide the large space into smaller ones. Then the entire panel, including the illustration board, was painted. Either enamel undercoat or gesso will do. Some of the areas of illustration board were then given an oil stain. To do this, thin either oil paint or enamel with paint thinner or turpentine. The decorative work, in lines and squiggles, was added with a metal cake decorator filled with a synthetic spackle or putty. "Dap" brand is a good, fine-grained one. The spackle is squeezed out very much the way you would to decorate a cake. After the frosting-like decorations have dried, the lines may be further stained with your thinned oil color. See Figures 4-3 through 4-10 for a step-by-step description.

It is easier to "antique," or stain, the decorative spackle lines after they are finished than to pre-color the spackle.

Figure 4-28. "Me on a Horse," 5 inches. Made at age six by Lizabeth Laury. (Tom Hurley)

C-55

C-56

C-57

C-58

C-59

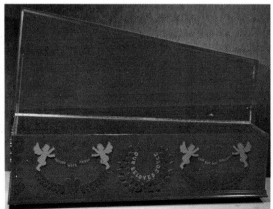

C-60

C-61

C-62

Figure C-55. "Collector's Item," 30 inches by 30 inches. Plywood provides a base, and pine stripping is used for the dividers. Horizontal divisions are made first. Then the vertical lines are cut separately and placed in a random arrangement. By Jean Ray Laury.

Figure C-56. Inscription for the "Ultimate Nostalgia Box," in cut wood appliqué. By Joyce Aiken.

Figure C-57. "Nostalgia Box," 16 inches by 20 inches, made from ½-inch pine in 3-inch-wide boards. It was designed especially to hold a collection of personal treasures. By Jean Ray Laury.

Figure C-58. "Blue Box," 8 inches by 20 inches. A blue stain over the wood, along with blue fabrics, set off objects in reds. By Jean Ray Laury.

Figure C-59. "Yellow Box," 15 inches by 15 inches. Wood stain combines with golds and yellows in a panel containing only objects in that same yellow and gold color range. By Jean Ray Laury.

Figure C-60. Small wood boxes, 3-inch cubes, are assembled on a backing panel 11 inches by 11 inches. Some boxes are left open to hold objects. Others are used as solid cubes with objects on the surface.

Figure C-61. A craftsman's coffin — made for her own (eventual) use! Six feet long. By Joyce Aiken.

Figure C-62. "Valentine," 24 inches by 30 inches. Blocks of wood, covered and appliquéd to a backing, provide areas to embellish with wood cutouts. By Jean Ray Laury.

For greater color contrast, the entire door can be given a coat of colored paint. This should be done after undercoat, or gesso, has dried. The step-by-step photographs demonstrate the use of tissue paper to give the backing a solid color. Other panels, shown in Figures 4-16 and 4-17, have similar work done with spackle on painted wood. Before tackling a full-scale door, try this technique on some smaller panels.

Unpainted hardwoods are used in the sun cutouts by Patricia Hopper in Figures 4-18 and 4-19. Intricate and careful cutting was required on the individual panels. Walnut was sanded to a smooth polish for the 11-inch squares and the squares were then appliquéd to the background with glue. The sun provides the theme, and the variations are used

once on each side of the door. The finished door is seen in Figure 4-20.

All of these approaches used on doors are applicable to other surfaces. The hollow-core door itself makes a good ready-finished backing for a large wood appliqué. Doors are not quite so overwhelming a project as they might seem at first. If this work is new to you, avoid having to tackle the design of a huge area. Divide the larger areas into smaller ones, which are easier to handle. Just the counterplay of circles on squares with various colors or natural woods can become a surprisingly complex and personal design. Remember that it is not necessary to excel in drawing. Some of the most stunning doors were created through variations of color and simple shapes.

Figure 4-29. "Cat."

5. Nostalgia Boxes

Nostalgia boxes, or any display of collections to which we attach our sentiments, are among the most intriguing of all wood projects on which to work. The compartmentalized boxes offer a means of singling out, and sharing, small objects for exhibit. The box itself, and the overall color pattern, carry the major part of the design so that the individual objects can be precious and detailed, or trivial and abundantly nostalgic. It puts only a minor emphasis on each item so that the absurd, humorous, intriguing, or eye-catching "things" can be presented. It is an irresistible invitation for a friend to share in this flickering box-by-box adventure.

Start out by doing a very simple nostalgia box — preferably using a ready-made box for the basic form. Drawers from an old sewing machine make great display boxes. Some may be arched, as in Figure 5-1, and others may be rectangular, but have ornate handles or drawer fronts. The proportion seems to invite a figure, and an apple doll took up residence in this one. See Figure 5-2. Turned on its side, the box could accommodate a series of smaller objects.

Soft-drink cases, shown in Figures 5-1 and C-53 (page 77) provide ready-made divisions of a good usable size. The box with a sliding door, Figure 5-3, contained a man's cologne, and the box behind it was constructed especially for the purpose of displaying a collection. Building the boxes yourself allows for areas of just the right size to accommodate the particular junk you wish to treasure. Or you could have a cabinetmaker provide you with boxes to your specifications.

Figure 5-1. An old sewing machine drawer and a soft-drink crate are good beginnings for nostalgia boxes.

Nostalgia boxes begin from either of two directions. You can start out with a collection and build boxes to display it; or you can first locate the boxes and then figure out what to put into them.

Various small wood boxes can be collected to form a larger area. The boxes can be stained dark (if they are raw wood), or painted (if they already have a finished surface). Then backgrounds can be covered with panels of felt. These are cut to size and glued in place. Other fabrics work well, depending upon the kind of activity and the texture desired. Velveteens or velours give an elegant touch, but those made with cotton fabrics will be easier to handle. Grosgrain ribbons, printed fabrics, photographs, and colored papers will all work. Felt is simpler to work with than most fabrics because it has a finished edge and will not ravel. Figure 5-4 shows how the felt is cut and inserted into the boxes. Do all the cutting and placement first, and when you arrive at a color arrangement that pleases you, the fabric can be glued into place.

Figure 5-2. Painted and lined with felt, the drawer provides a display case for an apple doll.

Figure 5-3. This nostalgia box was built from ½-inch thick and 2-inch-wide pine boards for a special collection. The "boxes" were then lined with colored felts. The small box was a drugstore discard that provides a good basis for a "peep show." By Jean Ray Laury.

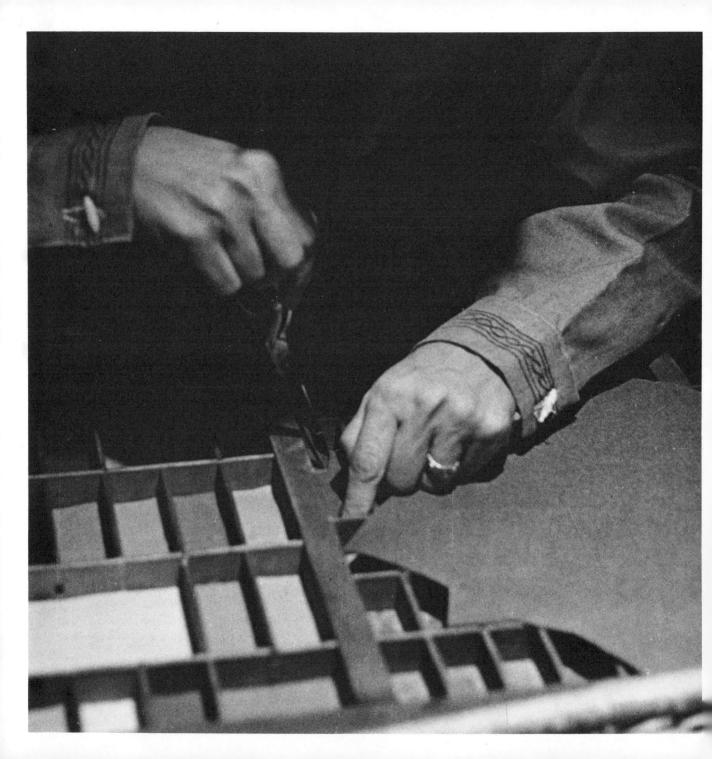

Figure 5-4. Felts are placed on top of the boxes to help determine color choices. Then cut strips of felt are inserted. All colors are arranged before any are glued, thus making it possible to alter the arrangement if necessary.

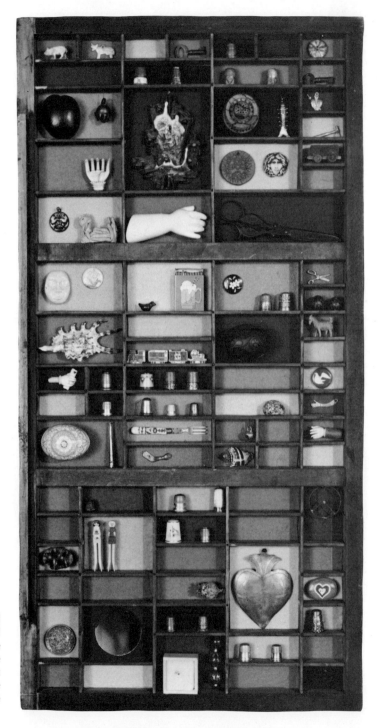

Figure 5-5. After all the felts are placed and glued, objects are added. Some are attached at the top, to hang free. Others rest on the base, or floor, of the box, and some are attached to the background felt. This box included hands, thimbles, and hearts. Some open spaces allow for the collection to change and grow. By Jean Ray Laury.

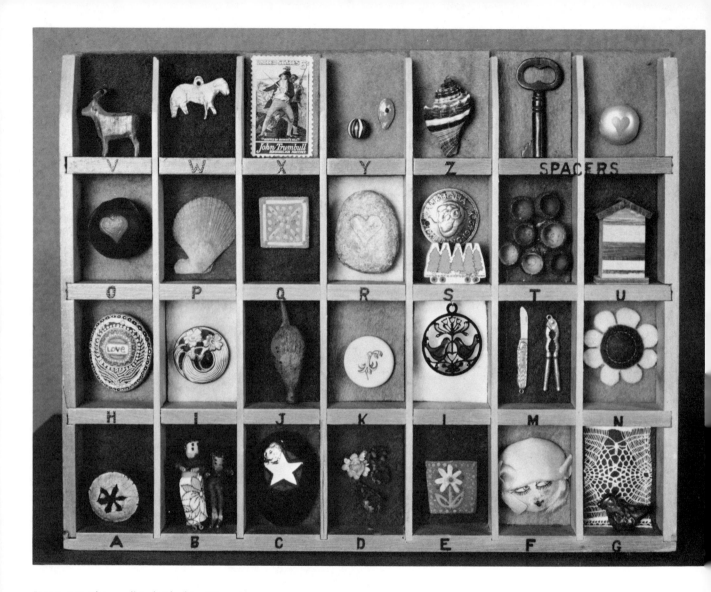

Figure 5-6. The small individual partitions in this type-case are 1⅛ inches by 1½ inches, which makes possible the display of delicate, tiny treasures. By Jean Ray Laury.

A collection of thimbles and other small objects is displayed in a ready-made box shown in Figure 5-5. This one is an old typesetter's case. The wood was left natural and dark, with the smaller areas filled with bits of bright color. If the box itself is dark, then bright colors work well in the recessed areas. A dark object will need a light color behind it if the object is to show at all. By playing with the contrast in value and color, your treasures can be given more, or less, prominence.

A lead pencil can be cut into short lengths to provide "posts" on which the thimbles sit. The advantage of using the posts is that the thimbles are kept in place without having to put any glue on the thimbles themselves. To keep thimbles from sliding out of place in this panel, small wood cylinders from a child's bead-stringing set were glued to the shelves. Any similar thing will do. You will devise various similar means of attaching pieces without damaging the objects with glue. Sometimes a nylon leader (fishing line) is used to sew, or tie, an object onto a piece of fabric or wood. Then the fabric, or wood, is glued into place. Another small typesetter's case was used in Figure 5-6.

Silverware trays also make good display boxes. Thrift shops often have them. Additional spaces can be made by cutting thin pieces of wood, or illustration board, to serve as dividers.

Figure 5-7. Nostalgia Box (detail). Photographs and box tops combine with three-dimensional forms in this box collection.

Figure 5-8. "Fresno." Nostalgia-box collection, commissioned for the entry to the Redevelopment Agency of Fresno, combines objects, photos, and drawings relating to the city's past, as well as its future. 48 inches by 48 inches. By Jean Ray Laury.

Figure 5-9. Various objects must be tried and sometimes discarded until you find the most satisfying arrangement. Try to find a large table which is not in use, as the clutter may remain for days.

Nostalgia boxes are simply constructed, beginning with a plywood base. It is easiest to use a 2½- or ⅝-inch-thick plywood base, then frame it with ½ inch by 2 inch pine stripping. A butt joint will be easier than a mitered joint for corners, especially if you have no miter box to use. Once the frame is in place, use additional pieces of the pine stripping, which is cut into lengths to go across the width of the box. These can be glued into place with any wood glue. Make the spaces between these vary so that not all the boxes will have the same height. When these have set, cut the vertical dividers to slip in between the horizontal ones. This allows for some necessary variation in the sizes of the individual boxes. The entire box can then be stained before any fabrics or papers are added. If you have been messy with your glue, it will really look stained. Stain cannot soak into the wood where there is glue on the surface.

Figure 5-11. ''Nostalgia Box.'' Crochet, needle-lace, mirrors, and paper all provide intriguing background for objects. 16 inches by 20 inches. By Jean Ray Laury.

Figure 5-10. Glue, paints, fabrics, pieces of wood, boxes — all can become a part of the collection. All the shells, and stones, and seeds you have carefully gathered, only to tuck them away in forgotten corners, may finally get the attention they deserve.

93

Figure 5-12. "The Ultimate Nostalgia Box."
Detail from the front, showing some of the
cherubs, birds, and festoons that elaborately
decorate the box. By Joyce Aiken.

While staining the boxes is simple, painting is more difficult — especially if you wait until after the box is constructed! If you prefer paint and want bright solid colors, it would be easier to paint the boards before the box is assembled. Then, after assembly, you need only touch up with the paint.

A panel commissioned for the Fresno Redevelopment Agency is shown in Figure 5-8. The plywood backing was about 4 feet square. When this was framed and the shelves were set in place, stain was added and the overall color pattern worked out. In this collection, all things relating to the historic, ethnic, and cultural background of the city were used. Finally, a clear plexiglass panel was used to cover the face, making it dust-free and tamper-proof.

Another approach to the box panel is shown in Figure C-62 (page 80). In this, a plywood backing was cut for the base, but instead of dividing it into boxes, areas were built up. Squares of plywood, or board, from ¼-inch to ¾-inch thick, were covered with felt and then attached to the backing panel. Some areas of the plywood were left flat; others built up to any of several different thicknesses. When all of the "boxes," or squares, were finished and in place, a frame was added. Finally, the objects were added to the blocks. The framing should always be done before the collection of objects is attached, since the whole panel has to be tipped and turned to add the frame. The objects are attached by glueing, sewing, tacking, or any other method that will work.

Whatever approach you use, the objects you select should relate in some way to one another. This may be through color, through sentimental value, or through the ideas they represent. It helps to have a good accumulation. Spread it out so that you can see all you have to work with. Drawers and cupboards can be emptied of those odd assortments of shells, buttons, or seed pods. Even an old postage stamp that particularly caught your eye could be licked into place.

Probably the ultimate in nostalgia boxes is the coffin. My friend Joyce Aiken has designed her own, feeling it would be outrageous for a craftsman to be buried in a standard chrome and steel container. Cherubs bearing garlands, and hearts and messages adorn the pink and red pine box. A detail in Figure 5-12 shows the varying thicknesses of the wood cutouts which were enameled and attached to the box. Figure C-61 (page 80) shows the box in its full glory.

Many of the boxes discussed in this chapter are shown in color on pages 77 and 80. While all variations of cutting, painting and appliquéing wood are absorbing and satisfying, few seem to be more intriguing than nostalgia boxes. They are not unlike patchwork quilts, with their blocks of various colors, each embellished with some decorative form. Others seem reminiscent of apartment windows at night — each offering a brief glimpse of things that seem familiar but go unnoticed.

Anyone with a touch of the pack rat or pocket-gopher in his nature will find new dimensions for his proclivity to collect, gather, and accumulate. Treasures and trivia alike form the complex focus of the nostalgia boxes.

Figure 5-13. "Heart."